Pearls of the English Language

Peter Harvey

Illustrations by
Alison Litherland

Lavengro Books
English language usage made plain

This book is published by
Lavengro Books
C/Gomis 43, 1-6
08023 Barcelona
Spain

www.lavengrobooks.com
books@lavengrobooks.com

Pearls of the English Language
ISBN: 978-84-617-4712-2
Spanish legal deposit: B 20456-2016
Text copyright © Peter Harvey
Illustrations copyright © Alison Litherland
Published by Lavengro Books
First edition 2014
Second edition 2016

Cover by Peter Harvey following a design by Alex Martín Ros.

All rights reserved. No part of this publication may be reproduced, stored in a retrieval system, or transmitted, in any form or by any means, electronic, magnetic tape, electrostatic, photocopying, recording, mechanical, or otherwise, without the prior permission of the copyright-holder in writing.

Intellectual property rights are protected under Articles 270ff of the Spanish criminal code and legislation in other countries. Legal action may be taken to defend the author's rights.

Applications to photocopy or scan this book or any part of it should be addressed to the Spanish reprographic rights agency CEDRO through the website www.conlicencia.com.

PEL2.0.1 September 2016

Contents

above & over; below & under, abroad & foreign, accents, ago, since & for, a lot of, much/many & plenty of, (al)though, despite & in spite of, American English, any, Arab, arrive
born
capital letters, chess, Christmas, city, town & village, clock & watch, colours & languages, comparative & superlative (form), comparative & superlative (use), could & was able
dates, do, double consonants, double negatives, draw
efficient & deficient, e.g. & i.e.
fare, future, future continuous, future perfect
gender & sex, glass, go + -ing, going to, group nouns
h, had had, have, hear, hot, house & home
in case, indefinite article, -ing form, in, on & at, irregular plurals, irregular verbs, -ise & -ize, its & it's
jam & marmalade
kill
lie & lay, long
means & series, modal verbs, morning, afternoon & evening
negative infinitive, no & not, number, numbers
often
passive voice, past continuous, past perfect, past simple, past simple & present perfect, people, place names, playing cards, prepositions with home, prepositions with time, prepositions with transport, present continuous, present perfect, present simple, prize, programme, public
quiet & quite, quotation marks
relative clauses, remember & forget, remind, rise & raise, road
schwa, search (for), see, sensible & sensitive, shall & will, silent letters, since, singular 'they', street & lane, stress difference
tasty, temperature, that that, to + -ing, travel, try
used to
want etc. somebody to do something, wash, weak vowels, weigh & weight, weights & measures, whom
youth
appendices: 1 phonetic symbols; 2 irregular verbs

Introduction

As the name of the book suggests, Pearls of the English Language consists of concentrated pieces of concise information about the English language that are intended to help people who are learning it. They are written and presented in a form that makes it easy to assimilate and remember them.

Each Pearl contains the basic elements of the point that is being made. They cannot include all the details and exceptions, and are not intended to do so.

More complete information about these points and many more aspects of the English language can be found in *A Guide to English Language Usage*, also by Peter Harvey and published by Lavengro Books.

This book describes British English with some notes on American usage.

A Kindle version of this book is available.

I must thank *Alison Litherland* for the illustrations. Her artistic work can be seen on her website www.alisonlitherland.com.

About Peter Harvey

I have spent many happy years teaching English. I have worked in Germany, Zambia and Saudi Arabia, but I have spent most of my life teaching adults in Spain.

I enjoy explaining the English language to people who want to learn it and am pleased to reach a wider audience through my books.

He who would search for pearls must dive below.
John Dryden

A
above & over; below & under

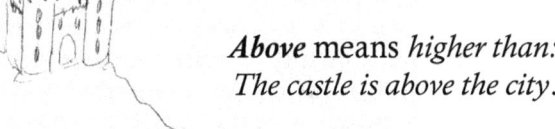

Above means *higher than:*
The castle is above the city.

Over means *vertically above:*
The lamp is over the table.

Clearly, anything that is over something is also above it.

Over and *under* are used with numbers:
Under 18 years.
Over 3,000 people.

We say *above average* and *below average.*

Below and ***beneath*** mean *lower than:*
The city is below/beneath the castle.

Under and ***underneath*** mean *vertically below:*
The table is under(neath) the lamp.

Beneath means *of lower value:*
That idea is beneath my consideration.
She married beneath her. (She married a man of a lower social status.)

abroad & foreign

Abroad is an adverb. It means *to* or *in another country*. You can *go abroad* for your holidays or you can *live abroad*.

Foreign is the adjective relating to other countries e.g. *foreign languages* or *foreign money*. The Foreign and Commonwealth Office handles the UK's foreign affairs.

It is not written *foreing*. It is not a word ending in *-ing*.

A *foreigner* is someone from another country.

A *stranger* is a person that you do not know. This is not the same as a foreigner. It has nothing to do with their nationality or country of origin or residence. It does not suggest that this person is strange in the sense of being unusual.

accents

English words do not have accents or other marks These characters are not found on English computer keyboards.

They are sometimes written on foreign words used in English such as *cliché, façade* and *mañana* where they affect the pronunciation, but often they are just omitted completely.

ago, since & for

Ago says how far back in the past something happened:
She arrived ten minutes ago.

Since /sɪns/ relates a state or action in the present or past to its starting point. It is used with the present perfect or past perfect:
I have/had been waiting since ten o'clock.

For gives the duration of an action that is continuing, or is completed, or is in the future:
They have lived in London for two years (using present perfect because they live there now).

They lived in London for two years (using past simple because they do not live there now).

I'll be living in London for two years.

See FUTURE CONTINUOUS; PAST SIMPLE & PRESENT PERFECT.

a lot of, much/many & plenty of

A lot of is used in all kinds of sentences:

I've got a lot of time.
Have you got a lot of books?
I haven't got a lot of time.

Lots of can be used instead of *a lot of*.

Much, which is uncountable, and *many*, which is countable, are usually only used in negative sentences and in questions as an alternative to *a lot of*:
I haven't got much time.
Have you got many books?

In affirmative sentences they are rather formal:
I have given much thought to it.
Many people believe it.

They are used with adverbs:
Too much, so much, very many.

Plenty of suggests an amount or number that is more than enough. *I've got plenty of money* does not mean that I am very rich. It means that I have more money in my pocket than we expect to spend this evening so we do not need to go to the bank to get more.

(al)though, despite & in spite of

(Al)though is a conjunction:
I went out (al)though it was raining.

Both *although* and *though* can be used in such sentences. There is no difference between *though* and *although*. These words are interchangeable.

Even though is emphatic:
I went out even though it was raining.

Despite and ***in spite of*** are prepositions:
I went out despite the rain.
I went out in spite of the rain.

Despite and *in spite of* can be used equally. There is no difference in meaning between them. They are interchangeable.

American English
There are differences between British and American English but they are not very great. The main grammar differences in American English are:

- the use of the past simple with *just (I just arrived)* for British present perfect *(I have just arrived)*
- *gotten* is sometimes used as the past participle of *get*.
- no preposition is used with days: *I'll arrive Monday* for British *I'll arrive on Monday*.

There are a few minor spelling differences including:
GB/US
-our/-or (colour/color)
-re/-er (theatre/theater)
-ogue/-og (dialogue/dialog)
-ce/-se (defence/defense)
axe/ax
plough/plow
tyre/tire

There are some important differences in vocabulary but there is no great difficulty in communication.

More complete information is available in *A Guide to English Language Usage*.

See DATES; PREPOSITIONS WITH TIME; PROGRAMME.

any

The *any* /'enɪ/ forms *anybody, anyone,* and *anything* are used as the object in questions and negative sentences. It is important to remember that they are not negative themselves and must be used with a negative particle:

Did you see anybody?
I didn't see anybody.

The negative forms are *nobody, no-one* and *nothing:*
I saw nobody.
I knew no-one.
I heard nothing.

When *any* is used as the subject of an affirmative sentence it implies that all are possible without restriction.

Anybody will help you is the opposite of *Nobody will help you.*

Arab

Arab is the adjective used for the people and culture, and is the nationality noun:
My neighbour is an Arab.

Arabia and *Arabian* refer to the Arabian peninsula.

Arabic is used for the language. It is the only case in English where a language name is different from the nationality adjective.

arrive

Arrive describes position, not movement. It can only be used with prepositions which describe position, basically *in*, *on* or *at*. It cannot be used with *to:*

He arrived in the pub before me.
but
He came to the pub by bus.

We arrived at the airport an hour before take-off.
but
We travelled to the airport by taxi.

Other prepositions can be used, for example *on, over, next to:*
The plane arrived over Paris at 12.30.

B

born

Your *birthday* is the annual celebration of the day on which you were born. You do not give the year when you say when your birthday is.

Being born is the passive form of *bear-bore-born:*
Shakespeare was born in 1564.
The baby will be born in May.

The verb can be used actively:
She bore her first child at the age of 16.

We talk of *women of childbearing age*.

Your *date of birth* is the date on which you were born, including the year.

When *bear* is not connected with birth, the past participle is *borne:*
The tree has borne fruit.
The costs will be borne by the agent.

Waterborne diseases are transmitted in water and when a plane is in the air it is *airborne*.

See DATES; PASSIVE VOICE.

C

capital letters

Capital letters are used for proper names. including the names of days and months. It is impossible to imagine *Tuesday* or *September* written with a small letter.

Words derived from proper names have capital letters: nationality adjectives and names of languages for example, and also words that come from personal names such as *Darwinian, Marxist, Thatcherite*.

However, usage varies and with time such words tend to lose their capitalisation.

A B C D E F G
H I J K L M N
O P Q R S T U
V W X Y Z

chess

The pieces used in chess are *king, queen, bishop, knight, castle* or *rook*, and *pawn*.

When the king is under direct attack it is in *check*. When it cannot escape that is *checkmate* and the game is ended.

A position where neither player can win is called *stalemate*. This word is also used to refer to negotiations that are not moving.

Christmas

Christmas Eve is 24 December.

Christmas Day is 25 December.

Boxing Day is 26 December.

The name is not connected with the sport of boxing. In the 19th century people spent Christmas Day with their families and gave their presents on the following day. These presents were called Christmas boxes and for that reason the day became known as Boxing Day.

New Year's Eve is 31 December.

New Year's Day is 1 January.

Eve refers to the whole day, not only the evening: *I'll phone you in the morning of New Year's Eve.*

city, town & village

A *city* is big and economically important. Traditionally the definition of a British city is that it has a cathedral.

The *City of London* is the financial centre, not the whole metropolitan area. It is completely surrounded by the rest of London but has its own municipal council and police.

A *town* is an important administrative and commercial centre but it does not have the independence of a city.

Historically, towns had markets and were the seat of local government and the law courts.

A *county town* is the judicial and administrative centre of a county. It is called a county town even if it is a city.

A *village* is smaller than a town and has little power for itself. It has a church.

A *hamlet* is very small with a few houses or farms. It probably does not have a church.

clock & watch
A *clock* stands independently on a table, or is on the wall of a building, or is part of a computer, DVD player, mobile phone etc.

A *watch* is carried with you, on your wrist or in a pocket. At one time there were *pocket watches* as well as *wristwatches*. Now the word *watch* is normally used alone.

colours & languages
The names of *colours* are used as nouns without articles:
Blue is my favourite colour.
This is a nice green.
The correction is marked in yellow.

The names of *languages* are also used as nouns without articles:
She speaks good German.
Her German is good.
German is not an easy language to learn.
She speaks German well.

See ARAB.

comparative & superlative (form)

Comparative and superlative **adjectives** are made with *-er* and *-est* respectively for one syllable adjectives:
Bigger, older, quicker.
Biggest, oldest, quickest.

Adjectives with three or more syllables have *more* and *most:*
More interesting, most difficult.

Adjectives with *-y* change to *-ier* and *-iest:*
Easier, funniest.

Adjectives with *-ful* take *more/most:*
More helpful, most hopeful.

Present and past participles must have *more/most:*
More tiring, most crowded.

Other two-syllable adjectives vary in form. Many can take *-er/-est* or *more/most*. If you are not certain, use *more/most*.

Adverbs with *-ly* have *more/most:*
More quickly, most smoothly.

Early, an adverb that is not made from an adjective, makes *earlier, earliest*.

comparative & superlative (use)

The *comparative* form of adjectives and adverbs is used when two things are being compared directly:
Mary is taller than Anne.
Mary works faster than Anne.

The comparison is made with *than*, which is only used in comparative sentences.

The *superlative* is used when three or more things are being compared:
Mary is the tallest girl in the class.
Mary works the fastest.

The superlative is usually associated with the preposition *in:*
The tallest mountain in the country.

or with *on:*
The tallest mountain on the island.
The smallest picture on the wall.

With time expressions we use *of:*
The hottest day of the year.
The last week of the holidays.

could & was able

Could refers to a general ability in the past:
He could always persuade people to give him a discount.

Was/were able is used for one particular occasion:
Because I negotiated well I was able to get the price reduced by 10%.

In the negative there is no difference:
After negotiating for three hours I couldn't get the price reduced at all.
After negotiating for three hours I wasn't able to get the price reduced at all.

In passive verb forms *be able to* is not used:
On that day alone tickets could be bought at a 10% discount.

D

dates

Dates are written in several different ways.

Day month year: 8 May 2015 or *8th May 2015*. This is the common form in Britain.

Month day year: May 8 2015 or May 8th 2015. This is much more common in the USA.

When the date is written in numbers, the *DD-MM-YY* form is usual in Europe: *08-05-15*. However, *MM-DD-YY* is standard in the USA: *05-08-15*. This can lead to confusion when the day is 12 or less. It is important to be careful when reading dates written as numbers.

do

Do (present) and *did* (past) are the auxiliary verbs used for making questions and negative sentences:
Where do you live? I do not live here.
Where did you live? I did not live here.

They are used for emphasis in affirmative sentences:
I do live here; I did live here.

Do can also be a main verb so sentences such as these are perfectly possible and correct.
I do do a lot of work; I did do a lot of work; What do you do?; Do you do a lot of work?

How do you do? is a formal greeting. Both people say the same. There is no answer. It is not a question about your health.

See HAD HAD; THAT THAT; WEAK VOWELS.

double consonants

A *hat* is something you wear on your head. *Hate* is the opposite of love. A hatter makes hats and a hater is someone who hates.

The *e* in *hate* is not pronounced but it changes the pronunciation of the *a* to a diphthong. It can only work back through one consonant so the *tt* in *hatter* blocks it, protecting the pronunciation of the short vowel.

This rule applies to all vowels. It is why *write* and *wrote* with diphthongs have one *t* but *written* with short /ɪ/ has two *t*'s.

There are very few exceptions to this rule. They include
dove /dʌv/
have /hæv/
live (verb) /lɪv/
driven /drɪvn/
gone /gɒn/
done /dʌn/
one /wɒn/ or /wʌn/

vowel	short	diphthong/long
a	æ	eɪ
e	e	iː
i	ɪ	aɪ
o	ɒ	əʊ
u	ʌ	juː

double negatives

Unlike many languages English does not use double negative words to reinforce negative meaning.

It is true that double negatives can be found in Shakespeare but a construction such as *I didn't say nothing* is regarded as incorrect in modern standard English.

There are special cases where double negatives cancel each other as they do in mathematics:

'Why did you say nothing at the meeting?' 'I didn't say nothing. (It is not true that that I was silent.) *I asked two questions.'*

I can't not go to the wedding means that it is morally and socially impossible for me to choose not to go.

draw

Draw does not only mean *to draw a picture*. It means *pull, take* or *move*.

The cowboy drew his gun means that he took it from its case.

To draw the curtains is to open or close them.

You *draw money* from a bank account and you *draw beer* from a barrel.

You *draw someone's attention* to a matter that is important.

An injury that *draws blood* is one that makes you bleed.

The noun is *draught* /drɑːft/.

Draught beer is *drawn* from a barrel.

A *draught* is a current of air passing through a room.

E

efficient & deficient

Efficient has two *f*'s but *deficient* and *proficient* have only one. *Suppose* has two *p*'s but *repose* and *depose* have only one.

The reason is that the Latin prefixes *ex-* and *sub-* were assimilated to the following consonants. There are examples with other prefixes, for example:
collateral / bilateral
offence / defence
suffix / prefix
oppress / depress.

e.g. & i.e.

e.g. (Latin for *exempli gratia*) means *for example:*
Tropical fruits e.g. mango, pawpaw and avocado.

i.e. (Latin for *id est*) means *that is to say* and introduces an explanation:
Tropical fruits i.e. those that grow in hot countries.

They are spoken and written as the names of the letters. The full Latin forms are not used but are given here for reference.

F

fare

Fare is an archaic word meaning *travel*. It is the money you have to pay in order to travel:
Bus fare, plane fare, train fare etc.

As a verb *fare* means *progress*, not travel:
How did you fare? (How did things go?)
I fared well. (Things went well for me.)

Fare is also a range of food:
Simple fare, good fare, coarse fare, usual fare, Christmas fare.

Farewell means *goodbye*, but it is only used when the people are separating for a long time or forever.

Welfare is a state of well-being. A *welfare state* is one that provides social benefits for its citizens.

See TRAVEL.

future

There are a number of ways of expressing the future in English.

They represent different ways of seeing what will happen and different forms can all be grammatically and logically correct with only a slight difference in meaning:

future continuous: *I'll be flying to Berlin on 10 January* (not surprising, normal course of events).

going to: *I'm going to fly to Berlin on 10 January* (intention).

will: *I'll fly to Berlin on 10 January* (prediction).

present continuous: *I'm flying to Berlin on 10 January* (plan).

present simple: *I fly to Berlin on 10 January* (schedule).

See FUTURE CONTINUOUS; FUTURE PERFECT; GOING TO; SHALL & WILL; PRESENT SIMPLE.

future continuous

The future continuous is used for an interrupted action in the future:
I'll be cooking dinner when you arrive.

It is used for a future that is unsurprising or in the natural course of events:
I'll be flying to Berlin on 10 January so I will take the packet with me.

See FUTURE; PAST CONTINUOUS; PRESENT CONTINUOUS.

future perfect

The future perfect refers to a time period that will continue up to a point in the future:
By Christmas I'll have flown to Berlin ten times.

See FUTURE; PAST PERFECT; PRESENT PERFECT.

G

gender & sex

Gender is the grammatical name used for classes of nouns: masculine, feminine and neuter. It is sometimes instead of *sex* to refer to social rather than biological differences, especially in feminist writing: *gender issues, gender studies* etc.

Sex is the biological difference between male and female animals and plants as found in their reproductive systems.

glass

Glass is the substance that windows are made of.

People wear *glasses* to help them see.

A *glass* is a container that people drink out of. We say that it is a *wine glass, beer glass, cocktail glass* etc. because they are all made of glass.

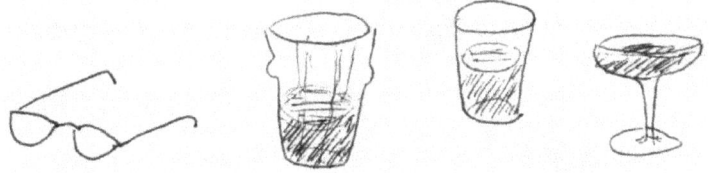

Sometimes glasses for drinking are made of plastic. The only sensible name for these things is *plastic glasses* even though it sounds strange.

go + -ing

With verbs describing a sporting or physical activity we use *go ...ing:*
I went swimming every day.
He goes fishing on Saturdays.

Some other verbs that are used with this construction are:

angling	*hunting*	*shooting*
cycling	*jogging*	*shopping*
fishing	*riding*	*skiing.*

See -ING FORM.

going to

Going to is one way of expressing the future.

It is used for intentions:
I'm going to fly to Berlin on 10 January.

It is used when there is present evidence that something will happen:
He's going to break the record. (His time is very good at present.)

It's going to rain. (The sky looks very dark.)

See FUTURE.

group nouns

Group nouns (e.g. *army, committee, team*) take either a singular or a plural verb depending on whether the speaker thinks of them as a single unit or as a collection of individuals:
Newtown United is the best football team in the country (thinking of one team).
Newtown United are playing Oldville Town on Saturday (thinking of eleven individual players).

In many cases there is little effective difference between the two forms.

Police always takes a plural verb:
The police have arrived.

See NUMBER; WEAK VOWELS.

H

h

In English the letter *h* is pronounced.

There are only three words in which it is silent: *heir, honour* and *hour*, and of course their derivative forms. With these words the indefinite article is *an*. We say *an heir, an honour* and *an hour*.

At one time the *h* was silent in words like *hotel, habitual* and *historical*, where the stress is not on the first syllable. This is still sometimes shown in print by the use of *an* with such words.

had had

Sometimes we say *had had*. This is correct in sentences such as *I had had a difficult time earlier in the year*.

This is the past perfect of *have*. The first *had* is an auxiliary verb. It has the weak pronunciation /həd/ or it becomes the contraction *I'd*.

The second is the lexical verb and has the full pronunciation /hæd/.

See DO; PAST PERFECT; THAT THAT; WEAK VOWELS.

have

Have got is used for possession:
He has got a big house.
Has he got a big house?.
He hasn't got a big house.

This is the present perfect of *get*. It is common in British English.

Have can be used with *do:*
He has a big house.
Does he have a big house?.
He doesn't have a big house.

This is found in British and American English.

Have is also used for actions:
I have eggs for breakfast.
I was having a shower when the phone rang.

hear

You *hear* something because the sound reaches your ears.

Hearing is involuntary: *I heard a noise.*

You *listen to* something with attention.

The *to* is used when the verb is transitive:
Listen to me.
Did you listen to what I said?

It is not used intransitively:
Listen!
I wasn't listening very carefully.

hot

As well as its usual meaning referring to temperature, *hot* means *spicy* with relation to food. A dish that is strongly flavoured with pepper or curry for example is *hot*.

This is a standard term used on restaurant menus and in the labelling of curry sauces.

The opposite to *hot* in this case is *mild*.

house & home

A *house* is a building that people live in:
They've bought a new house.
Our house has been painted.

Home is more personal and emotional. *My home* is not only the building. It includes everything that is associated with it.

Someone who is from a *good* or *bad home* has a good or bad family background.

See PREPOSITIONS WITH HOME.

I

in case

In case is a conjunction meaning that something is done as a precaution:
The sky's clear now but take an umbrella in case it rains later.
I didn't expect rain but I took an umbrella just in case.

This is different from *in case of* meaning *in the event of:*
In case of fire the building must be evacuated immediately.

indefinite article

The English indefinite article is *a* or *an* depending on the pronunciation (not the spelling) of the following word. The *n* has no grammatical significance.

This is a phonetic device to prevent two vowel sounds from coming together as for example in *a apple, a open door*, which would be difficult to pronounce.

We say *a university* or *a European country* because these words begin with /j/.

We say **an** *FBI investigation* and *an R&D department* because the names of these letters begin with a vowel sound.

-ing form

The *-ing form* is both participle and gerund.

The *participle* is used in continuous verb forms:
He is working.
I was cycling.

It is used in participle clauses:
Walking down the road I was caught in the rain.

The **gerund** is the part of the verb that operates as a noun:
Cycling is healthy.
I like cycling.
I have given up cycling.
I am tired of cycling.

Because the *-ing* form is a gerund and gerunds are nouns, the *-ing* form follows prepositions. Sometimes the preposition is *to*. We say:
I am looking forward to seeing you again.
I object to paying so much.

Using *to* + *-ing* is necessary and correct. It is not an infinitive with *to*.

See GO + -ING; TO + -ING; USED TO.

in, on & at

In means *inside: in the house, in the box, in Britain.*

On means *on the surface of: on the wall, on the table, on the ground.*

Something is *in a book* because it is inside it but it is *on page 38* or *on the cover* because it is on the surface of the paper.

If a coin is *in your hand*, your hand is closed and is containing it.

If a coin is *on your hand*, your hand is open and it is visible on the surface of your hand.

At shows a spatial relationship that is not *in* or *on:*
At a bus stop but *in the bus shelter* or *on the seat.*
At work but *in your office* or *on the third floor.*

See PREPOSITIONS WITH HOME; PREPOSITIONS WITH TIME; PREPOSITIONS WITH TRANSPORT.

irregular plurals

The commonest irregular plurals are:

man, men	*goose, geese*
woman, women /ˈwɪmɪn/	*tooth, teeth*
child, children	*louse, lice*
foot, feet	*mouse, mice*

See PEOPLE.

irregular verbs

Irregular verbs are identified by three parts: infinitive, past simple tense and past participle, e.g. *fall-fell-fallen*.

In some verbs two of these are the same: *bring-brought-brought* and in some cases there is no change: *put-put-put*.

In *read-read-read* the infinitive/present is pronounced /riːd/ and the past and past participle are /red/.

With two exceptions, *cost* and *quit*, irregular verbs come from the Germanic roots of English vocabulary and many have similar forms in modern German. If a verb is obviously from a Latin or French origin it will be regular.

There is a list of common English irregular verbs in APPENDIX 2.

-ise & -ize

In British English *-ise* and *-ize* are both used: *realise* and *realize*. It is a matter of choice or of publisher's house style.

In American English *-ize* is standard.

The reasons for this difference are complicated and a good case can be made for each form.

These words can only have *-ise:*
advertise, advise, arise, chastise, circumcise, comprise, compromise, demise, despise, devise, disguise, enterprise, excise, exercise, expertise, franchise, improvise, incise, merchandise, premise, prise (force open), *promise, reprise, revise, supervise, surmise, surprise, televise*.

its & it's

Its is the possessive of *it*. Like the other possessive pronouns *my, your, his, her, our, their* it does not have an apostrophe.

It's is the contraction of *it is* or *it has*. Like other verb contractions, for example *he's* and *she's*, it has an apostrophe.

J

jam & marmalade

Jam is fruit that has been preserved with sugar. It can be made from any kind of fruit.

There is an exception. *Marmalade* is made of oranges, or sometimes other citrus fruit such as lemons and limes. It contains pieces of the skin of the fruit.

Ginger marmalade, containing pieces of ginger, is sometimes found.

K

kill

Killing is not necessarily an act of deliberate violence.

People can be killed in natural disasters or in accidents. Smoking, drink or overwork can kill people.

L

lie & lay

Lie-lay-lain is intransitive:
Lie down.
He lay on the bed.

Lay-laid-laid is transitive:
Lay him on the bed.
I laid a waterproof sheet on the ground.
They are laying electric cables in the street.

To lay a table is to prepare it for eating.

Birds *lay eggs*.

Lie-lied-lied means *deliberately to say something that is untrue*. It does not mean that someone has made a simple, honest mistake. The noun is *lie: That is a lie*. A person who tells lies is a *liar*.

long

Long can mean *for a long time* in questions and negative sentences:
How long did you live in that town? Not long/Long enough/Too long.
I hadn't been waiting long when the bus came.

In an affirmative sentence we say:
I have lived here for a long time.

Before long means *soon*:
We'll know before long.

No longer means that something that was once the case is not so now:
They no longer live here.

M

means & series

These words have the *s* in the singular:
This means of transport.
A TV series.

They do not change in the plural:
Various means of transport.
Two television series.

modal verbs

Modal verbs have four special characteristics that distinguish them from other verbs:

They are followed by the infinitive without *to*.
We say *I can/must etc. go* but *I want/expect* etc. *to go*.

They do not have *s* in the third person singular:
He must go but *She has to go*.

They do not use the auxiliary *do* to form questions and negative forms:
Can you see me?
You must not do that.

They do not have all their parts. *Must,* for example, only has its present tense form. It makes its future, past and perfect forms with the appropriate from of *have to*.

Can has *could* as the past and conditional tenses but uses parts of *be able* to make other forms.

See COULD & WAS ABLE.

morning, afternoon & evening

The *morning* is the part of the day before 12 o'clock midday (*noon*).

Afternoon is strictly the time after this but lunchtime is often taken as the dividing point.

The *evening* is less precise. It begins at about 18.00 or perhaps when people arrive home from work and lasts until the time when people go to bed.

Times like 02.00, 03.30 are *two o'clock at night* or *half past three in the morning*.

See ARRIVE; HOUSE & HOME.

N

negative infinitive

The negative infinitive is *not to* + *infinitive*:
I hope not to be late.
You have a right not to be disturbed.

The auxiliary *do/does/did* is not used in negative infinitive forms. We do not say *I hope don't be late.*

no & not

No is the answer to a question, *yes* or *no*.

It is a determiner:
I have no idea.
There is no good reason to believe that.

Not is the word that makes other words negative:
Not now.
Not if I can prevent it.

number

In sentences such as *A large number of bicycles were in the road* the verb is plural because the effective subject is *bicycles*. It could be rewritten as *Many bicycles were in the road*.

However, in *The number of bicycles in the road was very high* and *The number of students was divided by two* the verb is singular because the subject really is the singular word *number*.

A number of ... has a plural verb. *The number of* ... has a singular verb.

See GROUP NOUNS.

numbers

Thousands are written with commas: *1,234*.

Decimal numbers are written with points: *1.234*.

A ***billion*** is a thousand million (10^9).

A ***trillion*** is a million million (10^{12}).

Ordinal numbers, *first, second, third* etc., are written *1st, 2nd, 3rd, 4th* then *21st, 32nd, 43rd, 54th* etc.

Superscript type (*1st, 2nd, 3rd, 4th* etc.) is often used but is not necessary.

Thirteen is *13*, ***thirty*** is *30* and so on. A *teenager* is between thirteen and nineteen years old.

Once is one time. ***Twice*** is two times, then ***three times*** etc.

O

often

Some people pronounce the *t* in this word and others make it silent. Both are correct. There is no regional or class distinction.

P

passive voice

The passive voice is made with *be* or *get* and the past participle.

It is used when the focus of attention is on the subject rather than the agent:
Othello was written by Shakespeare.

It is used when it is not possible, or desirable, or necessary to name the agent:
This wine is made in Germany.
The glass got broken.

It is widely used in scientific writing because it provides anonymity, focusing on the action rather than the actor.

past continuous

The past continuous is used for two actions that continued for a long time:
I was watching TV while Mary was cooking dinner.

It is used for an action that is interrupted by a sudden event:
I was watching TV when the phone rang.

See FUTURE CONTINUOUS; PRESENT CONTINUOUS.

past perfect

The past perfect is used for an event or state that happened before another one in the past:
I had known her for five years when I married her.
They had moved into their new house when Stephen was born.
We'd been waiting for two hours before they told us that the flight was cancelled.

It is often used with *already*:
I had already known her for five years when I married her.

See FUTURE PERFECT; PRESENT PERFECT.

past simple

The past simple is used for actions or states in a time that is completed.

The time is stated:
I arrived yesterday.
I wrote three emails this morning (said in the afternoon).

or is implied:
I played football at school.

or is clear from the context, in the narrative of a story for example.

See PAST SIMPLE & PRESENT PERFECT.

past simple & present perfect

The *past simple* refers to a completed time.

The *present perfect* refers to a time that is not completed, including a person's lifetime.

These tenses are used for living and dead people respectively:
Shakespeare wrote 37 plays. (Shakespeare is dead. He cannot write any more plays.)
J. K. Rowling has written 20 books. (She is still alive. She can write more books.)

Often a conversation starts in the present perfect and changes to the past simple:
'Have you ever eaten snails?' 'Yes, I ate them in Paris last year.'

See PAST SIMPLE; PRESENT PERFECT.

people

People is a strange word. It is plural. We say *25 people, many people, people are, people have*. For practical purposes *people* is the irregular plural of *person*.

However, it comes from Latin singular *populus* and is cognate with French *peuple*, Spanish *pueblo* and other similar words.

It can have its own plural, *the peoples of Europe* for example.

It is not normally used in the singular as *peuple, pueblo* or German *Volk* can be.

place names
Place names are used as adjectives: *Liverpool cathedral, Barcelona airport.*

Roman is used to refer to ancient Rome. Other forms such as *Neapolitan* (from Naples), *Parisian, Venetian* and *Viennese* are literary and romantic. They are not used in modern colloquial English to refer to the cities.

playing cards
The suits for playing cards are ♣ clubs, ♦ diamonds, ♥ hearts, ♠ spades.

Each suit has thirteen cards: *ace, two* to *ten, jack* or *knave, queen, king.*

Jack/knave, queen and *king* are known as *court cards* or *face cards.*

Some games use a *joker*, which is a card that can represent any other card in the pack.

prepositions with home
You *go/come home* or you *leave home* with no preposition.

You *set out from home* or you *head for home* and you *arrive at home.*

You *are at home.*

See ARRIVE; HOUSE & HOME; IN, ON & AT.

prepositions with time

In is used with periods of time: *in the morning, in July, in summer, in 2013.*

On is used with days and dates: *on Tuesday, on 30 June, on my birthday.*

At is used with clock time: *at two o'clock, at 3.57* and with holiday periods: *at Christmas* but *on Christmas day* and *at Easter* but *on Good Friday.* We say *at night.*

By sets a limit: *by ten o'clock* means that ten o'clock is the latest possible time.

Till and *until* have the same meaning. There is no difference between them.

See AMERICAN ENGLISH; IN, ON & AT.

prepositions with transport

We say *by bicycle, bus, car, plane, taxi* and *train* but *on foot* and *on horseback.*

With determiners we usually use *on:* o*n my bicycle, on a bus, on this plane, on every train* but *in John's car* or *in that taxi.*

Note that we use *on* (not *in*) with buses, ships and planes.

See IN, ON & AT.

present continuous

The present continuous is used for things that are happening now:
He is reading a book.

It is used for things that are temporary:
Mary's living with friends (till she finds a place of her own).

It is used to express a plan in the future:
I'm flying to Berlin on 10 January.

See FUTURE; FUTURE CONTINUOUS; PAST CONTINUOUS.

present perfect

The present perfect is used for actions, events or states that happened in a time that is not completed.

An action or event can be completed:
I have written three emails this morning (said in the morning).
I have seen the Taj Mahal (at some time in my life).

or a state can continue into the present:
I have always supported Oldville United FC.

See FUTURE PERFECT; PAST PERFECT; PAST SIMPLE & PRESENT PERFECT.

present simple

The present simple is used for states that exist in the past, present or future:

Trees have green leaves.

It is used for habitual or repeated actions. *He drinks tea* does not say whether he is drinking tea now.

It is used for things that are always true:

Water boils at 100° C.

It is used for scheduled future events:

I fly to Berlin on 10 January.

See FUTURE.

prize

A *prize* is won in a competition, lottery, game etc.:

An *award* is given for outstanding achievement by a group of people who decide who is to receive it.

A *reward* is given in return for good behaviour, for example finding and returning something that has been lost.

programme

Programme is British. ***Program*** is American.

However, *program* is standard form used in Britain in connection with computers.

See AMERICAN ENGLISH; STRESS DIFFERENCE.

public

A *public company* is one whose shares are owned by members of the public and are bought and sold publicly on the stock exchange.

A company that is owned by the state is a *state-owned* or *nationalised company*.

The initials *plc* stand for public limited company.

A British *public school* is a traditional private school. The first of these schools were founded in the Middle Ages and were open to any member of the public who could pay.

Now they call themselves independent schools in order to avoid confusion.

In the UK schools that are managed by the public authorities are called state schools.

Q

quiet & quite

These are different words.

Quiet /ˈkwaɪət/ means *still, undisturbed, peaceful, with little or no noise:*
A *quiet room, voice, weekend.*

Quite /kwaɪt/ means two opposite things.

1) fairly, partly:
Quite good, quite hot, quite interesting.

2) completely:
Quite impossible, quite different, quite alone.

In 1) the adjectives are gradable. That means that there are different degrees of goodness, hotness or interest.

In 2) they are non-gradable. Either something is impossible, different or alone or it is not. There are no degrees of the quality.

Quite so shows full agreement:
'He's a good cook.' 'Quite so.'

quotation marks

Single '...' or double "..." quotation marks can be used to mark direct speech and quotations.

Quotation marks are also known as inverted commas.

Double marks are usually used in handwriting for clarity but printers and publishers choose their own styles.

When direct speech is nested, single and double marks alternate:
He continued his story, 'I asked him, "What are you doing here?"'
or
He continued his story, "I asked him, 'What are you doing here?'"

It is very unusual to find direct speech or quotations printed in English with other marks.

R

relative clauses

In *defining relative clauses* the relative pronoun is *who* (for people), *which* (for things) or *that* (for both). These clauses do not have commas:
The man who/that sold me this car is my neighbour.
The car which/that is in my garage is a VW.

When the relative pronoun is the object the pronoun is *whom* or *that:*
The man who(m)/that I saw is my neighbour.
The car which/that I bought is a VW.

They can be used with no pronoun:
The man I saw is my neighbour.
The car I bought is a VW.

Non-defining relative clauses add extra information. They have *who* or *which* but not *that*. These clauses have commas:
My neighbour, who sold me that car, is rich.
That car, which I bought last week, is a VW.

See WHOM.

remember & forget

You *remember doing* something after you have done it and you have a memory of doing it:
I remember locking the door.

You *remember to do* something before you do it:
I remembered to lock the door.

Forget doing is always used with a negative verb. It refers to a time after you have done something and you have a memory of doing it.

I will never forget locking the door as I left the house for the last time.

You *forget to do* something before you should do it:
I forgot to lock the door.

remind

You *remind somebody to do* something:
He reminded me to lock the door.

or that they have to do something:
Can I remind you that you have to send me the information before the end of the month?

rise & raise

Rise-rose-risen is intransitive. It means *to move upwards*.

It is used for movement that that can be seen or measured:
The smoke rose from the fire.
The rocket rose in the air.

The sun, temperatures, prices, unemployment rates, speeds, currency exchange rates etc. can rise.

Arise-arose-arisen is used for movement that cannot be seen or measured. Questions, doubts, difficulties etc. arise.

Raise(d) is the transitive form for both: you can *raise a floor* or *raise a question*.

road, street & lane

Road and *street* are both used in urban areas.

In the country a *road* connects towns and cities.

A *street* must be in an urban area. It has buildings on both sides.

A *lane* is a small, narrow road in the country.

S

schwa

This is the name of the sound represented by the phonetic symbol /ə/.

It can be represented by all the vowel letters in English. It is always unstressed and is often very short. It is the minimum vowel sound that is needed to move from one consonant to another.

For example, it is the sound of *a* in *alone, or* in *forget* and *er* in *mother*.

See WEAK VOWELS.

search (for)

To *search for* something means *to look for something with a lot of effort*.

I have searched for my glasses everywhere.

To *search something* is to examine it thoroughly. The police can *search* a house or a person, or luggage in an airport.

In computing you can search a file or a website. A *search engine* is the program that does this.

See PROGRAMME.

see

You *see* something because the light that comes from it reaches your eyes. Seeing is involuntary:
I saw a flash of light.

You *look at* something with attention. The *at* is used when the verb is transitive:
Look at page 64.

It is not used intransitively:
Look!
I wasn't looking very carefully.

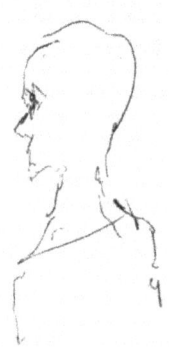

When you *watch* you pay close attention to something that is moving, for example a football match or a TV programme.

Watch can also imply vigilance. If I ask you to watch my suitcase, I want you to guard it while I am away.

To *stare* is to look at something without moving your eyes. It is rude to stare at other people.

sensible & sensitive

Sensible generally means *showing wisdom or common sense*, the opposite of *foolish*.

Sensitive means acutely affected by external stimuli or mental impressions.

shall & will

Will is the auxiliary verb for the future as a simple prediction:
I/you/he/she/it/they will fly to Berlin on 10 January.

Shall can also be used for the first person:
I/we shall arrive at 10 o'clock.

Shall is used in questions to make offers:
Shall I make coffee?

and to ask for suggestions:
What shall we do?.
When shall we arrive?

Will is used to ask for information:
What will we do?
When will we arrive?

Its contracted form *I'll* is used to make spontaneous offers:
(The phone rings.) *I'll answer it.*
'We need some bread.' 'I'm going out. I'll buy some.'

See FUTURE.

silent letters

The *b* is silent in *debt* and *doubt* and in words that end with *-mb* such as *bomb, comb, lamb* etc.

The *g* or *k* is silent in words beginning with *gn-* or *kn-: gnome, know* etc.

The *gh* is silent in *night, right* etc. and in *bought, caught* etc.

The *l* is silent in *talk, walk* etc. and in *calm, palm* etc.

The *p* is silent in words that begin with *psych-* /saɪk/: *psychology* etc.

The *r* is silent in *iron* /'aɪən/.

The *s* is silent in *island* /'aɪlənd/. It was first put in the word by mistake but is now required as the standard spelling of the word.

The *t* is silent in *fasten, listen* etc. and in *castle, whistle* etc.

The *w* is silent in *answer* and *sword* and in *who, whole* and *whore*.

See H; WEAK VOWELS.

since
This is pronounced /sɪns/, not /saɪns/ or /siːns/.

singular 'they'

The pronouns *somebody, anybody* and *nobody* are singular:
Somebody was in the house.

However, these words can be followed by forms of *they:*
Anybody who has lost their ticket will have to buy a new one.

This avoids the problem of having to use forms of *he or she:*
Anybody who has lost his or her ticket will have to buy a new one.

stress difference

Some words e.g. *compound, contract, finance, protest, rebel* have the stress on the first syllable when they are nouns and on the second when they are verbs.

In some cases there are differences in meaning between noun and verb.

A full list can be found in *A Guide to English Language Usage.*

See PROGRAMME.

T

tasty

Tasty refers to food that has a good taste and is pleasant to eat.

Tasteful refers to things that are in good taste in aesthetic terms or to appropriate behaviour.

Tasteless is used to give the opposite meaning for both words: *tasteless soup, a tasteless comment.*

temperature

Temperature is a measure of how hot something is but it also describes a body temperature that is higher than normal. If you *have a temperature* or *are running a temperature* you are ill.

Fever usually refers to a serious tropical disease, yellow fever, malaria, dengue fever etc.

See HOT.

that that

Sometimes we say *that that*. It is correct in sentences such as *I thought that that was the reason.*

The first *that* is a conjunction and has the weak pronunciation /ðət/. The second *that* is a pronoun and has the full pronunciation /ðæt/.

See DO; HAD HAD; WEAK VOWELS.

to + -ing

To is often used with the infinitive:
I want to go.
I hope to see you.

Sometimes it is used as a preposition with a gerund:
I object to paying so much.
I look forward to seeing you again.

I look forward to hearing from you is a common ending to a letter. It is polite because *look forward to* always refers to something pleasant.

See -ING FORM; USED TO.

travel

Travel is usually a verb.

The usual noun is ***journey***, whether long or short, a 24-hour train journey or a 10-minute bus journey.

Travel is used as a noun for the idea of travelling in general:
Travel agency.
Travel is educational.

Travels are long, adventurous journeys.

A ***trip*** is a return journey, typically for a few days. It includes all the time you are away, not only when you are travelling:
A three-day business trip to New York.

try

To ***try to do*** something means *to make an attempt*, to see if it will be successful:
I'll try to have the answer tomorrow.

To ***try and do*** something means the same but is less formal:
I'll try and have the answer tomorrow.

*To **try doing** something* means *to do it as an experiment* to see if it produces the required result:
Try putting less salt in it next time!

U

used to

Used to /ˈjuːstu/ or /ˈjuːstə/ with the infinitive describes an action or state that happened long ago in the past:
I used to play football on Saturdays.
I used to live in Liverpool.

It is only used in the past. In the present we use an adverb:
I often / usually play football on Saturdays.

For questions and negative sentences the recommended forms are *Did you use to play football?* and *I didn't use to play football.*

Used to with the -ing form means *accustomed to:*
I am used to working hard.

The passive of *use* plus infinitive is:
A mouse is used to operate a computer.

In this case it is pronounced /ˈjuːzd tu/ or /ˈjuːzd tə/.

See -ING FORM; LONG; TO + -ING.

W

want etc. someone to do something

We say:
I want/need/require/would like you to be here at 1 o'clock.

It is incorrect to say:
I want etc. that you are here at 1 o'clock.

We can say *I expect everyone to be here at 1 o'clock* and *I expect that everyone will be here at 1 o'clock* but they have different meanings.

wash

Washing does not necessarily involve the act of cleaning. Dirt is washed out of clothes and land, bridges, cars etc. are washed away by rain or flood water.

We even say informally:
I had a good meal washed down by a bottle of red wine.

To ***wash up*** is to wash the plates, dishes and cutlery after a meal.

A ***washing machine*** washes clothes. A ***dishwasher*** washes plates etc.

weak vowels

The English stress system has strong vowels and weak vowels.

Weak vowels are not stressed. They are shorter than strong vowels and are usually pronounced as schwa or are omitted completely so that letters that are written are not pronounced at all.

Examples of omitted vowels are found in the standard pronunciation of these words:
Catholic /ˈkæθlɪk/
corporate /ˈkɔːprət/
chocolate /ˈtʃɒklət/
different /ˈdɪfrənt/
history /ˈhɪstri/
interesting /ˈɪntrəstɪŋ/
police /pliːs/.

See HAD HAD; SCHWA; THAT THAT.

weigh & weight

Weigh /weɪ/ is the verb.

Weight /weɪt/ is the noun.

weights & measures

In Britain and the USA the metric system is not always used. The following metric equivalents are approximate.

length:
1 mile = 1.6 km
1 yard = 90 cm
1 foot = 30 cm
1 inch = 2.54 cm (exact)
1 nautical mile = 1.85 km

area:
1 acre = 0.4 ha
1 square foot = 0.1 m^2

weight:
1 stone = 6.35 kg
1 pound (1 lb) = 454 gm
1 ounce (1 oz) = 28 gm

volume:
Britain: 1 gallon = 4.5 l
1 quart = 1.1 l
1 pint = 0.57 l
USA: 1 gallon = 3.8 l
1 quart = 0.95 l
1 pint = 0.48 l

whom

Whom is the object form of *who* but it is rarely used. In questions we say *Who did you see?* or *I don't know who he saw.*

It is sometimes used with prepositions in very formal relative clauses:
The man with whom I had lunch but *The man I had lunch with* is more natural.

It is used with prepositions in very formal questions:
To whom did you send it?
but
Who did you send it to?
is more natural.

Y

youth

A *youth* is a young person, and in fact almost always a young male, but a group of youths could consist of both sexes.

As an uncountable noun *youth* refers to young people in general:
The youth of today are our future (always with a plural verb).
and the time when you are young:
In my youth.

Appendix 1: phonetic symbols

vowels
/iː/ see, sea, chief, these
/ɪ/ sit, hymn
/e/ bed
/æ/ cat
/ɑː/ arm
/ɒ/ hot
/ɔː/ born, Paul, walk, fall
/ʊ/ put, book
/uː/ moon
/ʌ/ run
/ɜː/ her, fur, sir
/ə/ See SCHWA

diphthongs
/eɪ/ day, lain, made
/əʊ/ no, know, rode, road
/aɪ/ my, die, high, ride
/aʊ/ how, house
/ɔɪ/ boy, boil
/ɪə/ near, beer, tear, here
/eə/ hair, there, tear
/ʊə/ poor, sure, curious

consonants
/b/ but
/d/ dog
/f/ few, photo
/g/ get
/h/ he
/j/ yes
/k/ cat, kid, quit, chemist
/l/ leg
/m/ man, bomb
/n/ no, know, gnome
/p/ pen
/r/ red, write
/s/ sit, city, psych-
/t/ top, missed
/v/ voice
/w/ we, wheel
/z/ zoo, plays, lives
/ʃ/ she, station, mission
/ʒ/ decision, measure
/θ/ thin
/ð/ this
/ŋ/ ring, ink
/x/ loch (Scottish)
/tʃ/ chip
/dʒ/ jar, judge
/ʔ/ glottal stop

Appendix 2: irregular verbs

This is a list of common English irregular verbs. A full list can be found in reference books such as my Guide to English Language Usage.

infinitive	past tense	past participle
be	was/were	been
bear	bore	born/borne
beat	beat	beaten
begin	began	begun
bend	bent	bent
bite	bit	bitten
blow	blew	blown
break	broke	broken
bring	brought	brought
build	built	built
buy	bought	bought
can	could	(been able)
catch	caught	caught
choose	chose	chosen
come	came	come
cost	cost	cost
cut	cut	cut
deal	dealt	dealt
dig	dug	dug
do	did	done
draw	drew	drawn
drink	drank	drunk
drive	drove	driven
eat	ate	eaten
fall	fell	fallen
feel	felt	felt
fight	fought	fought

infinitive	past tense	past participle
find	found	found
fly	flew	flown
forget	forgot	forgotten
freeze	froze	frozen
get	got	got
give	gave	given
go	went	gone
grow	grew	grown
hang	hung	hung
have	had	had
hear	heard	heard
hide	hid	hidden
hit	hit	hit
hold	held	held
hurt	hurt	hurt
keep	kept	kept
know	knew	known
lay	laid	laid
leave	left	left
lend	lent	lent
let	let	let
lie	lay	lain
lose	lost	lost
make	made	made
mean	meant	meant
meet	met	met
put	put	put
quit	quit/quitted	quit/quitted
read /riːd/	read /red/	read /red/
ring	rang	rung
rise	rose	risen

infinitive	past tense	past participle
run	ran	run
say	said	said
see	saw	seen
sell	sold	sold
send	sent	sent
set	set	set
shoot	shot	shot
show	showed	shown
shut	shut	shut
sing	sang	sung
sit	sat	sat
sleep	slept	slept
speak	spoke	spoken
spend	spent	spent
stand	stood	stood
steal	stole	stolen
swear	swore	sworn
sweep	swept	swept
swim	swam	swum
take	took	taken
teach	taught	taught
tell	told	told
think	thought	thought
throw	threw	thrown
tread	trod	trodden
wake	woke	woken
wear	wore	worn
weep	wept	wept
win	won	won
write	wrote	written

A Guide to English Language Usage for non-native speakers

... an entertaining and illuminating read ... shows a high awareness of learners' needs – it is clearly written by someone with solid classroom experience ... The grammar sections are a strong area of the book ... The information provided [on pro-nunciation] is accurate and relevant ... the cultural information as a whole is well-presented, colourful and accurate ... [it offers] clear and useful directions for learners
Modern English Teacher

Every English fact at your fingertips ... a more than handy reference tool for all involved in imparting linguistic knowledge on a regular basis. In the author's alphabetically arranged detailed content one can only admire the spirit of Dr Johnson ... it will help out when dealing with potentially awkward customers, or those keen to try out a new teacher.
ELGazette

When you start reading it, you are reminded of Modern English Usage by Fowler; however, in this case Peter Harvey is dealing with the reality of the foreign learner and what that learner wants to know ... A Guide to English Language Usage is a good reference book for all of us who are teaching and for advanced students as well. It is worth having in our libraries ... It is very practical, having been written by a teacher who knows his trade, and is highly recommendable.
TESOL Spain Newsletter

Not just a reference book explaining the intricacies of English grammar, but also a source of entertainment for the language-lover, covering numerous areas of the culture of the English-speaking world.
Dr Brian Mott
Department of English and German Philology
Barcelona University

Great English Mistakes made by Spanish-speakers (with a few Catalan specials)

An easy-to-read and user-friendly book ... grammar receives careful attention ... may benefit both intermediate and advanced students of English ... Teachers of English may also find it useful.

TESOL Spain

While [this book] is clearly aimed at the Spanish-speaking learner of English it is also valuable for the teacher of English working in a Spanish-speaking environment ... [it highlights] many of the false friends which exist ... Translations show the learner what words do, and, equally importantly, do not mean ... with a wealth of real-life examples which are sometimes humorous, the book is very readable ... There is certainly a gap in the market for such a book ... of all the many English language books I have on my bookshelf, this is the only one that has a long waiting list of Spanish-speaking friends wanting to borrow it.

Modern English Teacher

~~~~~~~~~~~~

For information about Lavengro Books including full reviews and samples go to www.lavengrobooks.com